These reliable books from Sandra Felton will help you "clean up your act."

The Messies Manual *The Procrastinator's Guide to Good Housekeeping* A humorous, perceptive guide for structuring all aspects of home life.

Messies 2 *New Strategies for Restoring Order in Your Life and Home* Warning: This book has been determined to be dangerous. Anyone who reads it will catch an overwhelming desire to look his or her best, clean out closets and drawers, organize files, wash dishes (before they resemble chia pets), and balance checkbooks.

The Messies SuperGuide *Strategies and Ideas for Conquering Catastrophic Living* Are you mired in Messiedom? Does the sound of the doorbell cause you to quake…break out in a cold sweat…or run and hide? Here are creative ideas and activities for bringing out the beauty you desire in your life and in your home.

Messie No More Enlightening, encouraging … serious yet gently humorous, this book abounds with hope for even the most hopeless Messie. Sandra Felton's practical strategies will help you put the Messie life-style behind you once and for all.

MEDITATIONS
FOR
MESSIES

*A Guide to
Order and Serenity*

Sandra Felton

Fleming H. Revell
A DIVISION OF
Baker Book House
Grand Rapids, Michigan

Unless otherwise identified, Scripture is from the King James Version of the Bible.

Scripture marked TLB is taken from *The Living Bible* © 1971. Used by permission of Tyndale House Publishers, Inc., Wheaton, IL 60189. All rights reserved.

Scripture marked NIV is taken from The Holy Bible, New International Version. Copyright © 1973, 1978, 1984 International Bible Society. Used by permission of Zondervan Publishing House. All rights reserved.

Library of Congress Cataloging-in-Publication Data

Felton, Sandra.
    Meditations for Messies / Sandra Felton
      p.   cm.
    ISBN 0-8007-5447-6
    1. Orderliness—Meditations.   2. Home economists—Prayer books and devotions—English.   I. Title.
BJ1533.O73F45   1992
640—dc20
                                                92-5474
                                                CIP

Copyright © 1992 by Sandra Felton
Published by Fleming H. Revell,
A division of Baker Book House
P.O. Box 6287, Grand Rapids, MI 49516-6287
Printed in the United States of America

THE MESSIES ANONYMOUS ORGANIZATION

Messies Anonymous is a fellowship of those who struggle with clutter and disorder in their lives. Sometimes Messies work on the program individually using M.A. principles and receiving help from the many books available. Many succeed in this way and find themselves changed and their lives freed from the burden of the messy life-style. Others feel the need to gather together in M.A. groups to find help for their common problem. All of us seek to fulfill the purpose for which we are put on the earth that is being hindered by disorder.

No organizational problem is beyond help. We focus on ourselves and the ways of thinking and feeling that got us into this destructive way of life. As the Messie begins to absorb the program, her life will begin to change slowly but surely. We learn this program by sharing and working the Twelve Steps* as they apply to disorder, not by the traditional educational process. In groups, we tell our stories, our hopes, strengths, fears, and insights into healing.

Whether you seek recovery in a group or individually, as you apply the principles of M.A. you will find the beauty, order, and dignity that you seek for your life.

*The Twelve Steps and Twelve Traditions of Messies Anonymous and the Twelve Steps and Traditions of Alcoholics Anonymous, on which they are based begin on page 115 of this book.

 # INTRODUCTION

As I Change

I am reading these meditations because I have a strong hope that my house and way of life will change from one of clutter, randomness, and stress to a life in which my house is beautiful and orderly, my time schedule under control, and my life gracious and harmonious.

Mixed with hope is fear that my old habits will overtake me in the midst of trying to change and wipe out my resolve, dashing my hope to earth.

I will take one day at a time. At the end of each I will applaud any improvements and leave failures behind.

I will start each day anew. In this way fears will be compartmentalized. I can handle it one day at a time.

Lord help me focus on this one day and do my best to fulfill my hopes so at the end you and I may rejoice together in the new life that is mine.

"Therefore do not worry about tomorrow, for tomorrow will worry about itself" (Matthew 6:34 NIV).

❦ How to Use These Meditations

You will find seven meditations in each section of *Meditations for Messies*. If you wish, you can read one a day and finish in fourteen weeks. But don't be discouraged if you skip a few days. Pick up again where you left off, and go on.

Meditations for Messies is also a book you can come back to time and again. Know that it's there for you. Turn to it on a day when you're having difficulty summoning the patience or focus your need to balance your life. Or on days when you can't "see the forest for the trees," you might turn to a Vision meditation.

These are key words for you to dwell upon:

Priorities

Focus

Beauty

Courage

Patience

Dignity

Vision

Each meditation guides you to reflect primarily on one key topic. As you put them all together and assimilate them into your life, you find the order and balance necessary for the building of a harmonious and gracious life-style.

At the end of each meditation is a spiritual reflection to use as the basis for a personal prayer. And, finally, you will find room for a brief personal reflection. Use this space to jot down some ways you can apply the day's meditation to your own household struggles.

Now proceed, one day at a time.

# PRIORITIES

The heavens themselves, the planets and this center
Observe degrees, priority and place.
                              —William Shakespeare

Priorities

The way of Messies Anonymous is the way to personal freedom. As with any other compulsion or addiction, we feel our lives are out of control. Our way of life is irksome and degrading. It is harder to face the situation when I realize that it is largely of my own making.

The temptation is to tackle the clutter, thinking that it is the primary problem. I may even hire someone to come into my home to organize it for me. Unless the change comes first in myself, my thinking, my feelings, it will be for naught. Slowly the house will again conform to my disordered thinking. I will only be discouraged by my inability to maintain what I long for.

I will do well to remember the words of the wise King Solomon, "As [a man] thinketh in his heart, so is he" (Proverbs 23:7).

Spiritual Reflection

Lord, I long for freedom from a way of life that degrades and crushes my spirit. Grant me the wisdom to see that both the making of the chains that bind me and the breaking of those chains are my own doing.

Personal Reflection

_____

_____

_____

_____

_____

Focus

It is very discouraging to get into a position of being overscheduled. Then there is no time for thinking, meditating, and resting. There's no time to do regular maintenance of the mind. When I overschedule, I feel as though I'm both losing a battle and betraying myself.

A basic change has come into my life. I used to enjoy being very busy. It gave me a sense of power. It protected me from taking time to think. I could pretend I didn't notice how bad the situation that I felt I had to control was. Time used to be my enemy.

Now that I have power to control my life, time is an ally. I know how to use it. I resent it when I don't have enough to keep my house and life in order. I will keep my schedule with diligence. My life fits into it. I don't want it squeezed.

Spiritual Reflection

Lord, help me to use time for being, not doing.

Personal Reflection

_____

_____

_____

_____

_____

_____

Beauty

It is a funny thing to recall how willing I was to be a victim. I was like a child. If I was asked to do a job, I automatically took that as a signal that it was predestined (by God?) as my job to do. I felt I could not foil destiny. I had been chosen. If someone died and left me things, I assumed it was my responsibility to take and keep them forever. Someone else had chosen for me to have them and I was powerless to resist.

In all these circumstances I trusted that my life would go all right without any direction or choices on my part. I think that I even thought that this approach was choosing the spiritual path of trust. My life became chaotic.

Then I woke up to my power and responsibility of choice. Not only *could* I choose: I *should* choose. Now if things go right or wrong, the responsibility is mine. In short, what happened to me was that I grew up.

As an adult, I have no excuse if my house is not in the condition I want it to be. The choice is mine.

Spiritual Reflection

Great God, you have chosen to give us choices. Help me to wear the mantle of that responsibility like the adult I am. Guard me from slipping back into the victim role.

Personal Reflection

_____

_____

_____

_____

Courage

Two boys took a shortcut home from fishing because it was getting dark. Part of their path led over a long railroad trestle that spanned a deep ravine.

Suddenly, they saw the bright light of the train behind them. They heard the engine and began to run for solid ground. The train was faster than they were. So the boys lowered themselves over the edge of the trestle, hanging on to the crossties as the long train rumbled over them.

After the train had gone, they held on until they could barely hold a minute more, yelling for help into the dark. To their amazement, they saw the flicker of an approaching flashlight. A man walked up to face them in the darkness. In the light, they saw that they had almost reached the edge of the trestle. The ravine was behind them. Their feet hung a foot or so from the ground. They had thought they were near death. Yet safety was closer than they knew.

Many experiences, including organizing, are like that. I fear more than I need to. Success is closer than we realize.

Spiritual Reflection

Lord, help me see the reality that success is closer than I can envision at this time, and let me draw courage from that thought.

Personal Reflection

Patience

I am committed to a moderate life. I will not follow my natural tendency to overdo in so many areas. When I have choices to make, I will always make the moderate one.

I will not try to do everything.

I will not try to keep everything.

I will not try to act as a historian or librarian.

I will not try to act as a newspaper clipping service.

I will not try to volunteer for everything good.

I will not try to help every person in the world.

Instead, I will define who I wish to be and live within those boundaries. Later, after I have set a moderate pace in those areas, I may drop some activities and add others. But never again will I feverishly try to do and be too many things, because that fractures and dissipates the really important thrust of life.

Spiritual Reflection

Drop thy still dews of quietness,
Till all our strivings cease;
Take from our souls the strain and stress,
And let our ordered lives confess
The beauty of thy peace.

—John Greenleaf Whittier

Personal Reflection

Dignity

What insanity is this? Just because I live in the house alone, why don't I feel it is important to keep the house up? I don't want to bother to put the toilet paper on the empty roller. I store things on window sills. I don't want to close drawers or cabinets because I don't want to have to open them again. I don't see the need to keep the dishes washed. I don't throw away the small papers that clutter the house. Why? Because it's just me here to know or care.

What insanity is this? My lack of caring for myself flows from lack of self-esteem and flows toward the same destination. As the house deteriorates around me, I can't find things. I can't have people in. And I don't want to come home myself. Eventually, living in this house is like walking hip deep in molasses, slow and unpleasant.

Spiritual Reflection

Lord, keep me from having to strain in order to care about myself.

Personal Reflection

Vision

What if I were not a messy person? Would I then be perfect? Would my marriage and family life be perfect? No. It is possible that the messiness I am battling is part of a larger picture.

In the solving of the messy problem, I need also to make efforts for success in other areas of my life. Perhaps I have very little self-control. Perhaps I am fearful. Perhaps I have a poor self-concept. If I have been neglecting the spiritual aspects of my life, I need to change. Perhaps I need to consider what part procrastination has in my life. Am I making every effort to be a good team member in my family?

The principles of Messies Anonymous, which emphasize moderation, strength, focus, motivation, priorities, and planning, will help me to become the person I now have a vision to become.

Spiritual Reflection

Lord, help me to realize that my messiness may be just one part of a larger picture on which I need to work.

Personal Reflection

 FOCUS

The best way to escape from a problem is to solve it.
—Brennan Francis

Priorities

As a matronly old cat was walking down the street, she stopped to watch a younger cat chasing her tail. Around and around she went, circling until she was exhausted, resting a moment, and circling again, chasing her tail. During one of her rest stops, the older cat asked the younger one what she was doing.

"Well," answered the young cat, "I have been to cat philosophy school. There they taught me that organization is the most important part of a happy life. I also learned that organization is found in the tail. If I can just catch my tail and hold on to it I will be happy."

"That's interesting," replied the matronly cat. "I have never been to philosophy school, but I, too, have learned that organization is found in the tail. I, too, have learned that happiness comes from being organized. But I have found that if I get my thinking straight and go about my business—a balanced plan of living—the organization in my tail automatically follows. Then I have happiness."

Spiritual Reflection

Lord, keep me from fruitlessly pursuing order while neglecting the things that coax it to me.

Personal Reflection

Focus

In my bathroom lives a skink, or that's what I call it. It's really called a gecko, a kind of lizard about two inches long. It's altogether unpleasantly slimy looking, with buggy eyes and snakelike movements. It is very fast. I am unable to catch it. And sometimes it ventures into my bedroom.

The result is that all my actions revolve around the possible whereabouts of this skink. I am afraid to wipe my hands on the towel lest he be in the folds of it. I look in my shoes before I put my feet in. I hesitate to lift a jar. Before I put my foot on the floor at night, I must turn on a light.

It's only two inches long, and I see it only every two or three days, but what an influence he has had over all my life!

I am so obsessed with this little guy that I can't focus on anything else. It occurs to me that there may be some small skinklike idea in my life that has just as powerful an influence. Could my chronic clutter be because of some malevolent ugly idea lurking in my brain, seldom seen but all pervasive?

I don't seem to be able to catch the skink. Perhaps I'll have better luck with my outlook.

Spiritual Reflection

Lord, give me sharp vision so I may spot the mental skinks that, though hidden, hinder my life so much.

Personal Reflection

Beauty

Step Three of the Twelve Steps says that we make a decision to turn our will and our lives over to the care of God as we understand him. I think this phrase, "the care of God," is one of the keys to recovery from clutter. If I truly believe that God will take care of me and of those I am trying so hard to care for, will I be freed from my compulsion to have so much and to do so much? If I truly feel that God is intimately involved in my life, that he loves me and that he wants to guide me into what is ultimately best for me, will I be able to relax the striving to constantly prove myself by frenzied creating and succeeding?

This step says that we made a decision. In truth, there are many repeated decisions to turn my will and my life over to his care. I need to turn my will and my life over to his care when I am afraid, when I am confused, when I am discouraged, or, hardest of all, when I am self-confident. In short, God's care frees me from my compulsively messy behavior and frees me to pursue my effort to take care of myself. No puny human effort on my part can match his.

Spiritual Reflection

God, who cares for me, let me sense your goodness. Let it flow into my life, sweeping aside those false efforts to meet my own needs.

Personal Reflection

Courage

> God, grant me the serenity
> To accept the things I cannot change,
> The courage to change the things I can,
> And the wisdom to know the difference.
> —The Serenity Prayer

What bold words these are and how I need them as I tackle the problems that cause my house to be disorganized.

I need *serenity* as I face circumstances that are beyond my ability to change. Perhaps one of the reasons I have so much trouble with making progress in my organizational life is that I spend too much time and energy working on things I cannot change. The more I fight them, the deeper in trouble I will be.

I need *courage* to change the things I can. No one knows how much courage I need to face my fears about getting rid of things. Sometimes I am so afraid I even keep the trash lest some "treasure" be hiding there by mistake.

I need *wisdom*. Perhaps the greatest wisdom is to know that I will make many mistakes as I take control of my life. Making decisions always involves risk. The worst decision of all is to avoid the possibility of making a mistake.

Spiritual Reflection

O God, you have serenity, courage, and wisdom. Share some with me in my need.

Personal Reflection

Patience

"Protect me from the things I want," writes Jenny Holzer, a trendy verbal artist from New York who uses messages as art in public places.

How does she know me? Has she seen my inner desires? Does she know how overwhelmed I become when the "want" urge kicks in?

The sad part is that the wants don't always reflect what I would really like to have in the clarity of daylight thought. Somehow beyond my rationality, like a drunk lured to a bar or a bulimic bingeing, I lose control over my choices and begin to pull things into my life. The worst part is that after it is almost impossible to get rid of them. I hardly chose to take them in. I can't seem to choose to take them out.

When I think I know what I want, part of protecting myself is to have the patience to take the time and effort to examine my want when I'm not feeling compulsive.

Jenny is right. Protect me from the things I want.

Spiritual Reflection

Lord, how can I pray about an area of such weakness? But I do.

Personal Reflection

Dignity

The first of the Twelve Steps of Alcoholics Anonymous says, "We admitted we were powerless over alcohol—that our lives had become unmanageable."

Some people may look at alcoholism and messiness in very different ways. Alcoholism is seen as a serious problem while disorder in the house is considered a minor problem, an annoyance, sometimes a joke. Undoubtedly, on a global scale, alcohol is a more devastating destroyer.

However, when I am humiliated daily by my own powerlessness over the control of my life and surroundings, the problem of disorganization is malignantly pervasive. Like the alcoholic, I know that I am powerless over clutter and my life has become unmanageable. Like the alcoholic, I must come to realize the full extent of the problem. Disorder is not a funny part of my endearing personality. It is an insult and a snare to my efforts at significance.

By accepting the first step, I dignify myself by reorganizing my problem, and I put myself in a position to recover.

Spiritual Reflection

Lord, help me accept the full extent of my problem so that I may begin on the road to change.

Personal Reflection

Vision

What an advantage I have over those who came before me. People of the past must have struggled alone all their lives to overcome clutter in their lives. Some may have succeeded alone. But I am sure that many did not.

Today I have help from so many sources to show me my way—books that direct in organizational techniques or that illumine my understanding about my problem and its solution. There are professional organizers who are possibilities for assistance. I have Messies Anonymous group meetings, if I wish, to provide personal support. The path out of my situation is a rough and sometimes steep one, but it is well lit.

I am grateful for that.

Spiritual Reflection

Lord, thank you for the helps that abound. Now I ask you to be the great and ultimate help so that I may be willing to use what is available. "God is our refuge and strength, a very present help in trouble" (Psalms 46:1).

Personal Reflection

_____

_____

_____

_____

_____

_____

 BEAUTY

If you get simple beauty and nought else
You get about the best thing God invents.
                              —Robert Browning

Priorities

The word *fulfillment* is like the words *fill* and *full*. Could it be that I am trying to find fulfillment by filling my life full of so many activities, so many hobbies, and so much stuff? I have too many talents, too many interests, too many responsibilities for any one person. Yet, I don't have fulfillment.

For too long I have searched in the wrong place for fulfillment. I have a feeling I am using things that I can gather and activities that I can do to fill a hole that no number of things external to myself can ever fill. I have used them as a substitute for real fulfillment. Until I find real fulfillment, I will continue to be tempted to look for those substitutes and wonder why they are never enough.

Gathering stuff and keeping very busy is easy. Finding real satisfaction is hard. Perhaps now is the time to stop looking outside myself for the satisfaction I seek.

Perhaps I yearn for my true self. And perhaps I yearn for something or someone higher than myself. Pascal, the French mathematician and philosopher, said that there is a God-shaped vacuum in every heart. Perhaps it is he I truly seek.

Spiritual Reflection

Dear Lord, keep me from looking in all the wrong places for that which truly satisfes. Help me to listen for that voice that leads me to true fulfillment so I don't have to keep gathering junk.

Personal Reflection

Focus

Being disorganized is not a moral issue. Cleanliness, or order for that matter, is not next to godliness. If my house is topsy-turvy it is not necessarily a reflection of my soul. It helps to separate these things.

But God is "a very present help in trouble." My disorganized life is one of my biggest troubles. Surely he knows and cares. The second A.A. step says that I came to believe a power greater than myself could restore me to sanity. Sanity, order, balance, harmony, peace—how I long for them.

If a person plays a game like basketball poorly, a good coach plus practice can help. I'm going to get all the teaching I can and, by God's grace, learn to be the best player in the household arena that I can for my good and his glory.

Spiritual Reflection

Lord, send lessons given by yourself or others so that I may play a winning game.

Personal Reflection

Beauty

Because order in my home involves other people so much, I must consider how they fit into the changes I am going to make. In my zealousness to create order and beauty, I must take into account the preferences and desires of others who live with me. I cannot simply impose my will on them. Nor can I create expectations that they must fill in order to keep our home beautiful.

Other changes such as losing weight, stopping smoking, getting clean from drugs or sober from alcohol are much more solitary changes—although in some ways they too involve the family group. And those changes do have something in common with the changes I am making.

In truth, although my family may be an important factor to help or hinder the housekeeping change, they cannot be the bottom line for change. I must choose to change and be responsible for my changes because I want to change my life. The choice for how my life works must rest with me.

When Pogo uttered those immortal words, "We have met the enemy and he is us," he was describing my situation.

Spiritual Reflection

Lord, keep my focus on me—the only place it can be if there is going to be permanent change.

Personal Reflection

_____

_____

_____

Courage

"Have a nice day," the clerks say again and again as they hand me my packages in the stores. Those words sound as though I have a choice about it—and indeed I do!

It is my choice to decide whether or not to do as the store clerks suggest and "have a nice day." I can decide to do the opposite and have a rotten day.

I know that one of the things that will give me a nice day is to control my life. It is unrealistic to believe that my life will be fully under control in every aspect, especially when I am just beginning the road to recovery. However, I can do a little every day to gain more and more control over my disordered life.

Today I will do something to bring order into my life, to have a nice day.

Spiritual Reflection

Lord, thank you for revealing the truth that my life is indeed under my control. What a responsibility and what a relief it is to know that.

Personal Reflection

_____

_____

_____

_____

_____

_____

_____

Patience

Our strengths work against us. Only talented people are given greater work responsibilities. Only creative people are tempted to tackle yet another wonderful project. Only cultured people, bright people, committed, doing people are lured to overdo by their own responses to opportunities. That is because they are so alive, so interested in so very much. Our own brightness will be our downfall if we are not careful.

I must be careful to measure out the day wisely, not heaping on so much that I crush the life out of it. If I am impatient to get too many things done, I will get nothing done well.

I must be careful to orchestrate my life. Unrestrained violins, or any other instrument overpowering the whole, ruins the music.

Spiritual Reflection

Lord, let me play the music of life well because I've only got one performance, and every day is an important movement.

Personal Reflection

Dignity

It is often not easy for the Messie personality to see the problem of disorganization clearly. My bad point, my messiness, contains so much that is good. And, in addition, my good points involve so much that is bad.

For example, the part of my personality that does not plan ahead often opens for me wonderful and unique adventures and experiences. Many Messies are afraid to organize their lives because they fear losing spontaneity.

Our strengths, as Messies, often add to our clutter problems. My intellectual part feels I must keep clipping books and articles. My creative part needs many, many supplies.

Our weaknesses can lead to positive things and our strengths can lead to negative. It takes clear thinking and strong resolve to untangle the issues involved. Only my keen desire to live a gracious life of dignity will enable me to do so.

Spiritual Reflection

Lord, sometimes I feel like a ball of confusion. I know you see clearly. Enlighten and guide me in untangling my thinking at the points where it will help me to improve.

Personal Reflection

Vision

It is amazing how a change of perspective can make a difference in how I view the problem I have with the house.

One Messie told of going on a spiritual retreat. She returned home, after having her soul beautified and uplifted, and the everyday clutter of her house pierced her soul like an arrow. The contrast of the beauty of her soul and the confusion of the house was painful. In her mind, she began to change on that day. Some part of the wall of denial cracked a little, and she saw things as they really were.

More insights came later until she began to feel that all the grasping she was doing was primarily because of lack of faith in God's infinite care to provide for her. She let go of her perfectionistic need to keep everything, in order to provide for herself or others in the uncertain future. To replace what she let go of, came a related faith that God would provide as needs arose.

The dam of fear broke and (as a result) clutter flowed from the house easily.

Spiritual Reflection

Great God, we are groveling on the floor for crumbs under the table when you have a banquet prepared above. Quiet the fears of us, your needy children, and open our eyes to your provision.

Personal Reflection

# COURAGE

Ye fearful saints, fresh courage take,
The clouds ye so much dread
Are big with mercy and shall break
In blessings on your head.
                    —William Cowper

Patience

In ancient times, sailors believed that while they were at sea they had to be wary of beautiful women called sirens. These lovely creatures sat on the rocks along the shore, singing to the sailors, trying to lure them to their death on the shoals.

When I try to chart my life, my time schedule, the order in my house, I am often lured away from my charted path by good things, beautiful things along the way. They call to me to forget my responsibilities and goals. How well I understand the sailors' temptations.

It takes a maturity of thinking, which I have up until now lacked, to prioritize my life *and stick to my goals*. There is a place for those wonderful things that distract me now but not until I introduce order into my life and take responsibility for maintaining it. Then there will be time to listen to the singing.

Spiritual Reflection

Lord, when the siren call comes, help me to listen to a higher voice.

Personal Reflection

Focus

"Ambivalence can ruin your life," writes Jenny Holzer, an artist, on New York billboards and benches.

But how satisfying ambivalence is. I tell myself that I am ambivalent because I am able to see both sides so well. I can't make a decision because I don't know the future. But as soon as I am able to see into the future I will decide. So I unconsciously wait for a revelation in order to make a decision. I move cautiously, even wisely, while others around me are rashly making decisions that they may later regret.

Others would do well to emulate my example, I tell myself, and not make so many decisions. They should sit sagely with me while questions pile up around us. We should consider each pile of decisions, mulling them over together.

While I am wise and cautious, they will not wait with me. Somehow they clear away their decisions, and their lives move on. What a shame. I hope they don't make a mistake. But, I wonder sometimes, could Jenny Holzer be right?

Spiritual Reflection

Lord, give me the courage I need to make decisions. It is so hard, and I lie to myself.

Personal Reflection

Beauty

Golfers use a technique for success that can apply in many areas of our lives. When they want their ball to eventually land far from where they are, they focus on a closer spot, which is in line between the ball and the far goal. If the golf ball reaches the intermediate goal on target, it will likely reach the far goal accurately as well.

If it is hard to aim for the far-off goal I have for my house, I will aim for the closer goals along the way. Today I will make up the bed. I will put away what I get out. I will finish one job before starting another. I will say "No" to myself and others in areas that are not in keeping with my priorities. To watch a perfectly executed golf stroke speed the ball in a graceful arc toward its final goal is to admire a thing of beauty. As we strive to create beauty in our lives we can remember that making many smaller efforts and achieving many short-range goals go into creating graceful beauty in our lives.

As I focus on those daily goals, I will day by day be closing in on the long-range one.

Spiritual Reflection

Lord, how nice it is that great and distant success can be gained from doing such small and present things.

Personal Reflection

Courage

"Out of the eater came forth the meat. And out of the strong came forth sweetness" (Judges 14:14).

As my needs are met, I am strengthened to meet the needs of others. Just as a nursing mother must be nourished herself in order to nourish her infant, so I who care for others must have been cared for previously myself. I cannot give what I do not have myself.

Women are nourishers. I must look well to my own health —physical, emotional, mental, and spiritual. Only then will I, the eater, be able to give meat to others.

And, from my strength, will flow sweetness.

The word of the day is *strength*—for the job of caring for myself and others.

Spiritual Reflection

Lord, in my world where disorder and confusion wear me out, give me the strength I need to go on. From that strength let sweetness flow.

Personal Reflection

_____

_____

_____

_____

_____

_____

Patience

It is very hard to maintain the high level of attention, interest, energy, and enthusiasm that it takes for me to keep a consistently orderly house. As a Messie, I fight an uphill battle with myself. This battle against my own distractibility, my own forgetfulness, my inability to notice things that are out of place, and my poor organizational skills begins to take its toll on my resolve.

When the fire of enthusiasm burns low I must learn not to give up. I know from experience that by waiting, resting, keeping up the minimum of bed-making and other small chores, I will eventually see my enthusiasm return. Above all, I must avoid guilt and despair during the dark period. These just interfere further with the process of recovery.

After darkness comes dawn. After winter comes spring. For me there are seasons of housekeeping. After the discouraging period, the season of optimism returns. Through highs and lows, the improvement continues.

Spiritual Reflection

Lord, help me, whether walking through good times or bad ones, to keep facing toward my goal.

Personal Reflection

Dignity

A stranger approached the mountain cabin in the cool of the late afternoon. On the porch sat the family. A hound dog lay asleep on the porch moaning and groaning in pain.

"What's the matter with your dog?" the stranger asked.

"Wal, he's lyin' on a nail," was the reply.

"On a nail!" the stranger exclaimed. "Why doesn't he move?"

"It don't hurt bad enough yet for him to bother."

Change is so hard that I have got to be in significant pain before I will even consider it as an option. With messiness I am aware that I can't change the house unless I change my thoughts, feelings, values, and much that has made my life significant. No wonder I am willing to hurt rather than bother to change. But I am not a hound dog on a nail. I am a human with dignity. I have God's plan for my life before me. How can I excuse my willingness to endure pain rather than bother to move?

Spiritual Reflection

God, help me to wake up to my pain. Help me to wake up to the changes I must make. But more than that, help me to wake up to your design for my life.

Personal Reflection

Vision

Sometimes I think I am weak, bad, undisciplined, lazy, or crazy for having this problem of messiness. But most of the time I think I am a very sane person. I am the most surprised of anyone that I am having this trouble. I seem to live a productive, normal life (it certainly is normal for me). And yet I leave a distasteful trail of clutter behind me.

Some experts say that people with problems like mine might be out of touch with themselves in important ways. Sometimes I suspect they are right. I *am* out of touch with some important feelings. On some basic level, I fear that I am not lovable or acceptable. I am not comfortable with my humanness, my frailty, or my fallibility. I am left with mixed feelings. One side of me feels comfortable and normal. The other side suspects that there is a strong, troubled current under the placid surface of my life. That current shows itself in messiness.

Yet, if the problem of messiness helps me to grow, to mature, and to change inwardly, perhaps it will end up being more of a blessing than the problem it seems to be. Perhaps it will help clear my vision.

Spiritual Reflection

O Lord, it's funny how things develop. My messiness is both a teaching agent and a problem. This is much too complicated for me. Please use me and straighten it out for me.

Personal Reflection

PATIENCE

Let nothing disturb thee,
    Nothing affright thee;
All things are passing;
    God never changeth.
Patient endurance
    Attaineth to all things;
Whom God possesseth
    In nothing is wanting;
Alone God sufficeth.
            —Teresa of Avila

Priorities

Cleaning and organizing the house are two different things. They are Siamese twins, separate but connected. Their lives are dependent on each other. Although many Messies are conscientious about cleanliness, it is unlikely that a messy house will be as clean as it would be if it were organized and orderly.

Of the two, it is more difficult to organize than to clean. A woman in the Panama Canal Zone had several maids who just dusted her piles. Organizing leads the way for true cleaning.

To have an orderly and supportive house, I must remember to give attention to both twins. The thought of having a clean house, a house where the bathroom fixtures shine, the furniture glows, the rug is vacuumed, and the windows gleam makes my heart sing.

I will invite the twins of order and cleanliness into my home and ask them to stay, not as guests, but as permanent and welcomed family members.

Spiritual Reflection

Lord, what a dream! Better yet, what a possibility! Help me have a clean and organized house.

Personal Reflection

_____

_____

_____

_____

Focus

When a compulsive gambler decides to stop gambling, he is still left with his debts to pay. When a compulsive overeater finds a program of eating normalcy, she still has her weight to lose. When an alcoholic finds sobriety, he still has the problems that he has created during his drinking.

So, it is not surprising that when I find a program that leads toward normalcy in life, I am left with the clutter and chaos of past years to deal with. This is to be expected.

Now, with courage, commitment, and moderation, I follow my program of cleaning up my house and life. I do not look back to the past with regrets. That only brings despair. I do not look to the pile of work ahead of me because that is disheartening. I only look to the one task before me in my program. I only look to the one day that I have now. Success will come as I follow my program.

Spiritual Reflection

Lord, give me confidence in the program even when my confidence in myself is nil.

Personal Reflection

_____

_____

_____

_____

_____

_____

Beauty

Women work just as much today as they did before the invention of modern conveniences. However, the type of work has changed. Modern work is less physical and more noisy because of the machines involved. I certainly do not want to return to the days of backbreaking labor. But somehow I miss what I imagine were some of the advantages of that life.

I miss the forced fellowship with family that washing dishes encouraged. The art of spinning seems appealing to me because of the twirling wheel, the pumping foot, and the reflection this encouraged. I miss handwork, like embroidery, which gave a person permission to sit and talk with other handworkers or simply to meditate.

I don't think I will return to hand dishwashing. I don't believe I will buy a spinning wheel or other charming, but impractical in today's world, contrivance. I *do* think I will look for some handwork and use my handworking time for reflection and contemplation—a kind of ordering of the soul.

Spiritual Reflection

Lord, give me time for strengthening contemplation. "As [a man] thinketh in his heart, so is he" (Proverbs 23:7).

Personal Reflection

Courage

Caterpillars turn into butterflies. But a caterpillar can't turn into a butterfly without going through the chrysalis stage, that in-between time when it is neither caterpillar nor butterfly. In the chrysalis stage the caterpillar melts into a helpless blob of goo as it reorganizes itself into a whole different animal. If I were a caterpillar-becoming-a-butterfly, I would not like that stage. As a matter of fact, as a Messie-becoming-a-successful-average housekeeper, I don't like the uncertain and unfamiliar stage that comes in between.

I am getting rid of my old way of deciding to keep everything but I don't exactly know how to decide what to get rid of. I have decided not just to pile everything on the table until later. But where shall I put my things? I have lost some of my old habits and my old ways of thinking and feeling. They have not yet been replaced with new ones.

Yes, the in-between stage is very uncomfortable. Someone has said you don't discover a new land without being out of sight of the shore for a very long time.

Spiritual Reflection

Dear Lord, I will be very, very glad when new ways are established, when I have developed new and orderly patterns. But no matter how hard the transition is, with your help I will not turn back.

Personal Reflection

_____

_____

_____

Patience

Those of us who are Messies frequently fail to realize that the reason we find it so hard to part with the clutter around us is that we derive so much comfort from it. We decided in some dim passageway of our past that if we couldn't organize our lives, at least we could fortify them by building a comfort zone of familiar and cozy, important and mundane things. They all serve as guideposts of events in our lives. Their very volume testifies to the fullness and importance of our path to this point.

I must try to remember that, comforting as my fortress of clutter is, it echoes back a very uncomfortable life-style. I call for comfort from my clutter. It sends back confusion. I call for significance from my "collection." It sends back frustration.

Could my life be improved by taking more to heart words of the Lord Jesus, "A man's life does not consist of the abundance of his possessions" (Luke 12:15 NIV)?

Spiritual Reflection

Lord, help me to open my hand full of collections so that I may grasp with it the order you have for me.

Personal Reflection

Dignity

Parts of my life have been left dormant. I know it is true. My ability to make beauty and order has been sleeping. Now I feel myself awakening.

Within my soul I feel a desire for a new way of life stirring. I feel not only the desire but the will to change within me.

I am opening my eyes to a different person. I am creating a new image of myself. I am a person of dignity and worth. Much of my clutter has been gathered and kept as an outflowing of disrespect to myself. Before, I served myself scraps on a paper plate at a graceless table. Now I expect quality served on china—with a rose in a bud vase beside it.

Slowly I am setting my thermostat of satisfaction higher. It is a new feeling and a good one.

Spiritual Reflection

Lord, how did I get in this way of thinking? Why have I been so disrespectful of myself? Better yet, Lord, how do I get out?

Personal Reflection

_____

_____

_____

_____

_____

_____

Vision

One of the chief differences between the Messie and the successful, average housekeeper is that the successful housekeeper has confidence in the future and her ability to handle it. The Messie fears being unprepared for the future. I keep things—so many things—because I fear that the future will deny me what I need. I keep so many papers and articles because I want to be armed with knowledge in order to outwit the onslaught of problems that may come.

Average, successful housekeepers are casual and comfortable about their needs in the future. They give away books and magazines, clothing, pots, and pans with aplomb.

"Look at the birds of the air; they do not sow or reap or store away in barns, and yet your heavenly Father feeds them. Are you not much more valuable then they? . . . Therefore do not worry about tomorrow" (Matthew 6:26, 34 NIV).

Spiritual Reflection

Lord, give me confidence that you will take care of my future so I don't need to sacrifice my present for it.

Personal Reflection

# DIGNITY

It is terrifying to see how easily in certain people, all dignity collapses. Yet when you think about it, this is quite normal since they only maintain this dignity by constantly striving against their own nature.

—Albert Camus

Priorities

What about others who live with me and who do not want to change the way the house is kept? They like it messy. Or, rather, perhaps they prefer leaving it the way it is rather than changing their own way of living to improve it. Sometimes the very people who complain most about the messy house resist what I am trying to do to make a difference.

This is not surprising. How long did I resist? Why should I expect that just because my time has come to change, theirs will come, too, at exactly the same moment?

To change myself is a very difficult matter. To change others is impossible. However, that does not mean the situation is hopeless. My own dignity requires that I continue to follow my own path to change. As the house begins to take on order and beauty, the resistant ones cannot help but be influenced.

I will not be deterred by resistance and lack of cooperation. The power of the changes taking place in me will work in ways I cannot now imagine if I am patient and consistent.

Spiritual Reflection

Heavenly Father, give me a single-minded resolve to do what I must do in order to change my life from clutter to order. But help me to go about it in a kindly and loving way when it involves dealing with others who do not share or respect my goals.

Personal Reflection

Focus

For a long time I did not understand the idea of "one day at a time." Somehow it seemed to be a negative approach that cut me off from yesterday and tomorrow.

Perhaps it is because I need the "one day at a time" concept so badly that I resisted it so much. It is my tendency to hold on tightly to the past. The past is sacred. It is where I store much of who I am. It is also my tendency to try to predict and prepare for the future. It is very hard for me to focus on "today."

And yet is it not abundantly obvious what a mess my unfocused life is causing me? While I hold on to the past and all of its paraphernalia and while I busily collect stuff to carry me safely into the future, my present life is miserable. In short, my life in principle is fine. In reality, it is rotten.

Focusing on the present, on today, means living fully in the only time I have got: *now*. It means sacrificing stuff from the past if it interferes with my life now. It means not keeping all that stuff that I or someone else might want if it messes up my life now. Now is all I have. The past is gone, as good or as bad as it may have been. The future may not ever arrive. But I do have now—wonderful, full, meaningful, *now*.

Spiritual Reflection

Great God of the present, help me to live, really live, in the wonderful present. Keep me from looking to the past for satisfaction or hoping that tomorrow it will get better. Help me to make a great now.

Personal Reflection

Beauty

Up until now my house has been such a practical thing, mainly a place to store things I needed and wanted—or thought I might. I have turned my house into a storage room, a museum, a library, an office, anything but a place of beauty and comfort. How did I ever become a high priestess to the practical?

Now I begin to see a little glimmer of beauty in my home. When I see that glimmer it gives me hope that I will be able to go on—pushing back the drive toward practicality, thinning out or eliminating altogether those mindless and endless collections that hang like an ugly albatross around my neck.

That glimmer of beauty gives me hope that my home, my home, can be aglow with loveliness that will comfort the inner part of me that yearns for it and will welcome all who enter.

Spiritual Reflection

Lord, break the chains of practicality at the points where it holds me back from beauty.

Personal Reflection

Courage

The change that I am making is a journey from innocence to awareness, from disorder to harmony, from powerlessness to control. I want to take control first over myself and then over my life. Like the journey of the tides, control and power flow in and out of my life. It is much easier to see the times when things are going poorly, when the tide is out. We note defeat here and there and think it will last forever. Yet, all the while our victory does not lie in our lack of defects but in our continuing to go on, stage by stage. In a way it is a blessed pilgrimage that I am privileged to make.

In the struggle to change, I grow. From my despair comes not only the possibility of success in my house but also of insight into myself.

Spiritual Reflection

Lord, hold my hand and guide my eyes along this journey. Give me strength because the road is sometimes so rough.

Personal Reflection

Patience

I will seek maturity. I have tried the other way and found it to be discouraging and unworkable.

Today I will seek to act appropriately in relation to the situation. I will not go to an extreme of lethargy or overactivity. I will balance my intellect and emotions so that my decisions will be wise, not driven by my unreasoning needs.

I will seek to see myself clearly, to develop both a proper self-image and a firm self-respect. I will respect others as I deal with them about the house or in other areas.

In short, I will attempt to do the right thing at the right time.

Spiritual Reflection

Lord, you who made a balanced and harmonious world, balance me.

Personal Reflection

_____

_____

_____

_____

_____

_____

_____

_____

Dignity

One of the reasons I continue to live a life of disorder is that I am willing to live chronically with more stress than most human beings would stand for. Sometimes I am proud of how much confusion and pain I can take. Sometimes I am even stimulated by my own crisis. But most of the time it makes me very tired and saps any zest for living.

Am I willing to live this way because I do not have enough self-respect to take care of myself? From now on, I will begin to be nice to myself by doing a few things to bring order to my life.

For example, I will have a place for my keys and purse when I come in. I will keep my makeup and nail file in a makeup bag. I will carry a car door key in my wallet so I will have a spare if I lock myself out. I will continue to look around my life to see if there aren't a few good things I can do for myself to make things easier for me.

Spiritual Reflection

Lord, help me to stop abusing myself. Place within me a solid sense of dignity and self-esteem that will not permit me to continue to mistreat myself with this way of life.

Personal Reflection

Vision

I often wonder how much of the real me my messiness is hiding. It seems to me that I got into this situation with the idea that I would be expressing myself to my fullest. But somewhere along the way something went badly wrong. The clutter ended up hiding me.

I thought I was starting out to be free of ordinary mortal constraints of order. Now I find I am in bondage to disorder. I thought I was providing for myself by keeping all this stuff and keeping it out in sight. Now I find I have deprived myself of a nurturing life in the most profound way. My own house is hostile to me. I thought I would keep everything so I could have what I needed. Now when I need it I can't find what I know is here somewhere.

It is time for me to wake up to the way things really are. I didn't mean to make them that way, but I did it anyway. Now the question is, what am I going to do to undo what I have done?

Spiritual Reflection

Gracious Father, I thought I was on one path. Now I find it led me wrong. Turn me around. Set my feet on the path of dignity, order, and beauty so that my real self, my higher self, can be seen. I am being crushed by this cluttered way of life.

Personal Reflection

VISION

The vision of things to be done may come a long time before the way of doing them becomes clear. But woe to him who distrusts the vision.

—Jenkin Lloyd Jones

Priorities

Jill is a fourth grade teacher. She spends every afternoon and evening grading the papers of her students. She can't straighten the house or cook dinner. Her husband, Bob, lives a bachelor's life except in the summer when she is off work. She is too busy to go out with him anywhere, even for a walk, during the school year. He cooks for himself. They have no children. Bob explains patiently that there is no alternative for Jill. "She teaches fourth grade," he explains. "She has to do it."

This year Bob wants to go home to California for Christmas. It is lonely, he says, with no family during the holidays. But Jill wants to stay home during her time out of school and clean house.

What does this have to do with messiness? Jill is a Messie for the same reason many of us are. She has turned herself into a machine, a dedicated, productive, even noble, machine. Cut off from her own feelings, she does not maintain intimate relationships with people or traditions. Pity Bob. But pity Jill more. Bob at least has himself. Jill does not. But she *is* a mighty fine teacher.

Spiritual Reflection

God, keep me from losing myself, my emotions, my intimacy, and my need for order and beauty in the mechanics of life. Give me the life you said I could have more abundantly. I don't want to settle for mere existence.

Personal Reflection

Focus

It is very easy to concentrate on the disorder in the house and to think only of it. It is the problem. It is the enemy. It is the focus. How discouraging. How fatiguing that emphasis!

If ever I could look beyond the clutter I would be surprised at what surrounds me. Outside the house, order is banging on the windows, hammering on the door trying to get in. It is slithering through the windows and flowing down the chimney. Order is aggressive and it wants me, my house, and my things. Until now I have successfully kept it out.

All I need to do is throw up the window sashes, fling open the doors, and it will surge in, pushing disorder before it until all is clear and fresh. Where will the disorder go? I haven't done it yet. But I will, and when I do I know it will somehow go somewhere.

Come in, order! Welcome! Do your thing.

Spiritual Reflection

Lord, outside I hear the banging of order. Give me the courage to open the house to its exuberant flow.

Personal Reflection

Beauty

There are two ways to solve problems. One is to attack each problem as it arises. The other is to set up an atmosphere in which it is difficult for the problems to grow in the first place. Obviously the second one is by far the best. Simply put: Don't kill the alligators. Drain the swamp.

I wonder how much of my struggle with messiness is because I am trying to attack individual problems while more are breeding behind me, multiplying faster than I can possibly get to them.

How can I drain the swamp in which my messiness flourishes? My swamp has many breeding pools. Messiness breeds in my desire to do everything perfectly, in my penny-pinching when it comes to the house, in my desire to do too many other things. I see so many other areas as well. My swamp is very big. Can I ever drain it? With commitment to do whatever it takes, yes! Without commitment I will be condemned to a life of fruitlessly killing alligators.

Spiritual Reflection

Lord, take my eyes off the distracting alligators and help me to see the swamp that nourishes them.

Personal Reflection

_____

_____

_____

_____

Courage

Maturity is the understanding that I must take responsibility for my own life. My situation is under my control. My hand is on the clay, and the piece forming before me is of my own doing.

I got myself into a disorganized state; it is my responsibility to get myself into a state of order. I have with me an arsenal of weapons for change. I will not become alarmed and run off in every direction at once. With deliberation and moderation I will use these weapons one at a time, slowly pushing back the disordered life that is my enemy.

I must remember, however, that this disorder is, in a way, not my enemy at all. It is my own creation that I made as an expression of my life at that time.

The point is: I am responsible for what my life becomes, ordered or disordered. The power is within my hands.

Spiritual Reflection

Lord, keep me from discouragement when I realize my responsibility or from haughtiness when I realize my power. Give me a sane maturity to do what I need to do.

Personal Reflection

Patience

Those who deal with alcoholism can be comforted with the idea that the alcoholic suffers from a disease from which he must have relief.

What about messiness? Is it a disease? From the surface meaning of the word *dis* (not) *ease* (comfortable) it certainly is a disease. Certainly, like a disease, I have something in my life that I don't want and that is hindering my living life as I want to. If I think of it as a disease it helps me detach from the self-recriminations and guilt that only discourage me.

Whatever it is, the solution is to heal myself by being honest with myself, by understanding my own characteristics and thoughts and by dedicating myself to whatever is necessary to reach that life of order and beauty which the dignity within me requires.

Spiritual Reflection

Lord, give me the wisdom to see my situation clearly and the courage and honesty to remedy it.

Personal Reflection

Dignity

The condition of my house cannot be allowed to be the source of my sorrow or joy. If I am happy only when my house is orderly, I am still enslaved. My joy and peace must come from balance I find within myself.

It is unreasonable to expect that things will always be under control. In addition to my weaknesses in the area of organization, there will be natural disasters or changes such as moving that will cause disorder and confusion in my environment. Even holidays will throw things off.

As I maintain my mental balance, the house will come around again. As I hold to the principles and practices that have served me well in the past, I can expect success in the future.

Spiritual Reflection

Lord, even when it doesn't seem to be working, keep me working the program.

Personal Reflection

Vision

Perhaps the worst thing about living a disorganized life is its harshness. Gone is the gracious and pleasant way of life that I long for. In its place are innumerable shocks and stresses caused by clutter and forgetfulness.

I picture the lives of others as a stroll in a beautiful manicured garden, with shady lanes and lovely vistas. My disorganized life is a rocky path in a harsh wasteland. Only one who has experienced it knows the stresses I have known.

King David prays, "Teach me your way, O Lord; lead me in a straight path" (Psalms 27:11 NIV). These are words of hope. We can be taught. We don't have to run around in circles. What a vision—to leave behind chaotic stumbling and walk with grace and dignity along a straight path.

Spiritual Reflection

Lord, deliver me from ups and downs, from unnecessary struggles brought on by myself. By your good Spirit, lead me on a level path.

Personal Reflection

_____

_____

_____

_____

_____

_____

 # PRIORITIES

Seek first his kingdom and his righteousness, and all these things will be given to you as well.
—Matthew 6:33 NIV

Priorities

Life is too short to read all of the novels I want to read, participate in all of the hobbies I want to pursue, enjoy all of the pleasures I want to feel, or learn all of the facts I'd like to know.

The desire to have all that I think is good, if left unchecked, will choke out my quality of life. A row of flowers in a garden must be kept thinned in order for each one to grow to its full potential. Too many flowers crowded together will press the life out of each other.

My life is just one chapter in God's overall book of history. I need to define the limits of my part in that story and develop it well.

The word for the day is *priorities*. What few things are important? I will do those well.

"Lord, help me to realize how brief my time on earth will be" (Psalms 39:4 TLB).

Whoever keeps doing the will of God will live forever" (1 John 2:17 TLB).

Spiritual Reflection

Lord, help me decide what few flowers I love best, and let me grow them well.

Personal Reflection

_____

_____

_____

_____

Focus

"One day at a time" is a saying that means much to those involved in Twelve-Step groups such as Alcoholics Anonymous, Al-Anon, and so on.

What does it mean to me, as a Messie? It means I won't concentrate on the mountain of work I must do and the millions of decisions I must make. Instead, I will focus on this one day and its activities. I will keep my focus there.

Just for today, I will close drawers after I open them. Just for today, I will work on the household project before me. And I'll finish one project before going on to another one. Just for today, I will not be discouraged about my situation. Just for today, I will treat myself with respect. I will allow and expect others to do things for me just as I do things for them.

Just for today.

Spiritual Reflection

Lord, just for today let me live with concentration on one thing at a time.

Personal Reflection

Beauty

It is true that ultimate change will come to my house when I change. It is also true that I cannot wait until I have turned into an internally organized person to begin changing my house. Actually, it is as I interact with the house that I see more clearly what issues I am dealing with.

As I attempt to get rid of things, I become aware of my insecurity. As I attempt to cut back on so many activities outside and inside my home, I notice how much I have defined myself in terms of what I do and not in terms of who I am. As I put things away in files or boxes or drawers, I sense my fear that I may not remember where they are or remember that they ever existed. As I drop some of the creative activities I love, it feels like dying—dying a little so that other parts of me may live more vitally.

Changing the house forces me to face myself. Then I can take better control of the house. The change is a circular process that spirals upward toward a sanely organized life-style.

Spiritual Reflection

Father, it would be easy to just understand the theory about changing without doing any changing. It would be easy, also, just to try to change the condition of the house without addressing the underlying issues. Neither approach alone will work very well or for very long. Help me to do both as wisely as I can.

Personal Reflection

_____

_____

Courage

I am, to quote Lincoln, "engaged in a great civil war." The war wages within my heart and mind.

How is it that a person with such high ideals as I have lives on such a low level in my own home? How is it that I, who can create such beauty in the arts and in crafts, manage to create such ugliness on the canvas of my house? Why is it that I am intelligent and successful in so many important areas of my existence but am as powerless as a child when it comes to simply organizing the things about me? I am zany and wonderful inside. But my house, which I hoped would reflect me, is drab and disagreeable. I who love people am forced to live in an isolated way because I am ashamed to have anyone in. I am afraid to get close to people for fear they will learn the truth about me.

It is the conflict between my values and my behavior that causes the pain of guilt, remorse, shame, and depression that is so much a part of my problem. The only way to bring peace to my life is to bring my level of behavior and my ideals into alignment. It sometimes seems impossible. But with God's help and the support of those who understand, I can find the courage to examine my ideals to make sure they're really mine, and then change my behavior to meet them.

Spiritual Reflection

God of peace, bring an end to this painful conflict by granting me victory in this battle within.

Personal Reflection

Patience

If I try to grasp too much of the Messies Anonymous program all at once, I may lose it all at once. I may lose it all. Being an overdoer, I may grow impatient and try to do too much, learn too much, change too much.

But as I slowly work the principles and practices, handling them one at a time in an orderly fashion, I will be surprised at how much I accomplish.

If I try to go too fast, I will become distracted and confused. As I apply the principles, things that are in a shambles will begin to straighten themselves out, slowly but surely. I must remember the maxim:

By the yard it's very hard.

But inch by inch, it's a cinch.

Spiritual Reflection

Lord, protect me from wanting to change too fast. I don't want to ruin my chances of success by starting to overdo even in trying to organize my life.

Personal Reflection

_____

_____

_____

_____

_____

Dignity

A woman was explaining to her companion that messiness was a problem only if others depended on you and your disorganization interfered with meeting their needs. If you could not send your children off to school with matching socks, or if their homework regularly got lost in the clutter, then it *was* a problem. But if you were the only one involved, she said, messiness was a "victimless crime."

How shortsighted was her view. She did not see herself as a victim of her own messiness. When I live in clutter I am the worst victim of my own disorganization. If I live alone, I alone am affected. But even if I live with others, my messiness is a significant problem because *my* life, *my* surroundings, *my* schedule, *my* peace of mind, *my* need of beauty, are important. The woman's statement indicated that she did not believe that her problems were worth considering.

If messiness is a "crime" and I am disorganized, then I am a significant "victim." And I alone am worth making a change for.

Spiritual Reflection

Lord, help me know that I am worth changing for.

Personal Reflection

Vision

Don't ever try to understand everything. Some things will just never make sense. Don't ever be reluctant to show your feelings. When you're happy, give in to it! When you're not, live with it. Don't ever be afraid to try to make things better. You might be surprised at the results. Don't ever take the weight of the world on your shoulders. Don't ever feel threatened by the future. Take life one day at a time. Don't ever feel guilty about the past. What's done is done. Learn from any mistakes you might have made.

Don't ever feel that you are alone. There is always somebody there for you to reach out to. Don't ever forget that you can achieve so many of the things you can imagine. Imagine that! It's not as hard as it seems.

> Don't ever stop loving.
> Don't ever stop believing.
> Don't ever stop dreaming your dreams!
>
> —Anonymous

Spiritual Reflection

Dear Lord, I'm grateful that there is so much more to life than the problems. There are solutions and joys out there for me! Thanks for the solutions, Lord.

Personal Reflection

 FOCUS

Let us strip off anything that slows us down or holds us back, and especially those sins that wrap themselves so tightly around our feet and trip us up; and let us run with patience the particular race that God has set before us.

—Hebrews 12:1 TLB

Priorities

The magazine advertised miniature brass trinkets and urged its readers to "recapture the beauty and grace" of a former time.

It occurred to me that the ad had spoken clearly to me about my attitutde toward keeping things. I keep many things because in them I am trying to recapture "the grace and beauty" of former times in my life. This battered piece was a wedding gift. That one belonged to my child. This one was from a vacation. That one was from a special person.

And so it goes. Each recaptures something for me—or used to. Now as they are gathered together they present themselves as so much clutter. Although I love the times they represent, they tarnish my present life. In the end, that tarnishes the memories as well.

Spiritual Reflection

Lord, keep me from being such a pauper in my present living that I feel I must always live in a richer past.

Personal Reflection

Focus

"One day at a time" is a slogan used by A.A. and Al-Anon. It is a good slogan for all who are making changes in their lives. As I change, I must not look at the past mistakes and losses that my disorganization has caused me and others. I must not look ahead with fear of the future or spend my time on plans that are out of my control because they are too far ahead.

It is part of my disability that I have difficulty focusing on one thing at a time, that I do not set boundaries for my thinking and attention. What a relief it is that I do not have to carry yesterday, today, and tomorrow all at once. All I need to carry is today—one day at a time. I don't even have to carry the whole day. I only have to concentrate on this hour, or more expressly, this minute.

If I concentrate on this minute and do my best now, the changes that I desire will occur.

Spiritual Reflection

Lord, thank you for packaging life into daily boxes. Let me stay in today's box and do my work there without trying to hop into yesterday's or tomorrow's boxes as well.

Personal Reflection

Beauty

It is true that order must come from the inside out. While I must concentrate on the inside part, I must also concentrate on working order into my daily life. Beauty will come from my complementary effort internally and externally.

I will look around at the house with a clear eye. Without panic or discouragement I will set my goals clearly. I will devise a reasonable plan and follow it. I will concentrate not only on what *needs* to be done but also on what I want to do to bring beauty and serenity into my new order. I will plan a reward for myself at certain intervals. I will follow my plan consistently.

In other words, I will work my outer efforts in harmony with my inner change toward control and order. As I do this I will find a balanced and harmonious life.

Spiritual Reflection

Lord, you see my heart but everyone else sees only my house. Give harmony in both areas so that I may find peace, beauty, and order without and within.

Personal Reflection

Courage

It is not a frequently told story, but it is not uncommon either. The headlines in the paper read, "Resident Dies as Fire Sweeps through Cluttered Condo." The article tells the story of a woman who is described as a "pack rat." She had so much stuff that she only had narrow aisles to walk through to get from room to room. The fire reduced her piles of paper, clothing, and other personal effects to four-foot piles of debris. Had she not had so much stuff she might have lived, the police said.

Few of us are in that extreme condition. We are not likely to perish in the same way this woman did. But each uncontrolled pile of clutter kills a little part of us. A little dies here with an incident of humiliation. A little dies there with a frustrating incident concerning a lost item. Death does not come quickly with one bite. Slowly our self-respect and hope are gummed to death. And then there are no headlines for the loss.

Spiritual Reflection

Lord, keep me from allowing myself to be killed so softly that all I notice is a creeping numbness to the possibilities of life as you offer it.

Personal Reflection

Patience

It is possible that in my desire for a life of order and harmony I may yield to the extremist within me, become so perfectionistic that I am discouraged despite the progress I have made.

I may have goals that are too high for myself, my family, and my house. The more discouraged I become, the more the program I am working falters.

Sometimes a realistic "less" is better than an unrealistic "more." In a reasonable way I will accept less if that will help me to reach my goal of order and harmony in the house and in my life.

Spiritual Reflection

Lord, help me leave behind neurotic compulsions and aim for a balanced approach.

Personal Reflection

Dignity

The importance of having an orderly and beautiful place in which to live is not so much in the order itself as in the part it plays in contributing to a complete and integrated life. My imagination flows clearer and more freely to completion; my passions for life, art, and love are purer and more controlled; and my caring for others is undistracted and wiser when my house is orderly and my activities are balanced.

Living a balanced life—filled with the grace notes of an orderly home, creative projects, and rewarding relationships—is not living a fragile life. Yet it can easily fall into disarray. I am responsible for keeping order and balance in my life. Disorder and dignity are mutually exlcusive.

A dignified life flows toward order. Order ebbs back to complement the dignified life. In the end, no one knows which is the source. No one cares which is the source when results are so satisfying.

Spiritual Reflection

Lord, I long for harmony. Grant me the vision to see the life possible for me.

Personal Reflection

Vision

I wonder what motivates me to want to get control over the disorder in my life. I expect that motivation varies somewhat at different ages and stages in our lives.

Perhaps those in early adulthood who want change want it because "it is right." They feel that adults take control. Of course, there are many who feel that they don't have to be orderly because they can handle the confusion. They don't yet know what a toll that will take.

Those in middle years want control for practical reasons. Their lives have become full of responsibilities that must be managed. In the later years, I suspect many disorganized people just want to find peace. Clutter assaults. They want to do something nice for themselves by moving out of it.

What are my motives? Some combination of all of these? Does it matter what my motives are? At some level, it doesn't matter *why* we want to have order. What is important is that we want it and that, when we begin to get it, we see that our lives are more reasonable, more fulfilling, and more pleasant.

Spiritual Reflection

Lord, sometimes I don't even know myself, my motives, my desires. They, like the rest of my life, are confused. If it is helpful for me to know, illumine me.

Personal Reflection

 # BEAUTY

Whatever is true, whatever is noble, whatever is right, whatever is pure, whatever is lovely, whatever is admirable—if anything is excellent or praiseworthy—think about such things.

—Philippians 4:8 NIV

Priorities

The Bible tells us that we cannot get fresh water from a well that has an intrusion of salt water. In more modern terms, computer experts tell us that you can't get accurate information out of a computer when you haven't put it in. Succinctly put, they say, "Garbage in, garbage out."

So it is with order in our homes and life. We can't draw order into our homes when our minds are in a state of confusion and turmoil. As a Messie, I am the last to realize how chaotic and disjointed my thought patterns are because they seem so natural to me.

In order to begin to make a change in my thought patterns, I will begin trying to work on one area. Today I will concentrate on a single task at a time and finish it before going on to another. Then from the well of my more focused life will flow a more focused home. "Order in, order out."

Spiritual Reflection

Lord, my life is awash with distractions. Center my thinking so that I may center my life.

Personal Reflection

Focus

It is important for me to understand that God is able to help those who call on him. The second step of A.A. says it well: "We came to believe that a power greater than ourselves could restore us to sanity."

If I am to find help it must be from God. I am not aware of the nature of my own needs or the reasons behind them. Working on becoming neat, as important as it is, is only the tip of the iceberg. God sees the hidden part of the iceberg where the real answers lie.

God can help restore me to sanity, if only I will let him. God can help me focus my attention and my energy on my problems and my solutions, one thing and one day at a time. I do not have to be perfect; I do not have to restore myself to sanity. All I have to do is to focus on the power greater than myself who can restore me to sanity.

Spiritual Reflection

Lord, in ways I can never know, you are the source of order and beauty in my life. You are the strength for change when I am weak, the motivator when I am discouraged, the beginning and destination for all.

Personal Reflection

Beauty

For one inexperienced in such things, creating beauty is not an easy task. When the house is in disorder and cluttered, I may have made fitful and sporadic attempts at bringing some sort of loveliness into my home. But the effort was short-lived as it became obvious that creating beauty amid clutter was impossible.

When order comes, beauty is possible. But I am not experienced in creating beauty. I hardly know my own preferences in colors or styles because I have been so cut off from that part of my feelings.

So now, it takes much thinking, looking in books, talking to those who know, buying and returning. Slowly and surely a special beauty of my own making begins to appear.

Like God in his creation, I see that it is good.

Spiritual Reflection

Lord, waken in me the long sleeping loves and tastes that lie within me. Grant me the wholeness that creating my own beauty supplies.

Personal Reflection

Courage

"Aren't people who live in messy houses just lazy?" people often ask. If they only knew how much I long for order and how much I would be willing to give for it, if only I could.

The word isn't *lazy*. People who live in clutter are *powerless*. Yes, I feel powerless to control my house, my feelings about my possessions, my family's habits in the house.

It is that impotence that is so frightening, so discouraging. And the ironic part is that I myself frequently call laziness what is actually powerlessness. And I berate myself for it.

I don't need guilt. I need comfort in knowing that I can find the power if I seek it in the right places.

Spiritual Reflection

Lord, comfort me in my powerlessness. But, even more, Lord, give me power over my life.

Personal Reflection

Patience

It is strange how much I am tempted to overdo. Perhaps the temptation to collect or commit to too many activities is greater than the temptation to collect too many items.

Surely it is more destructive. Items in the house put pressure on the house and my living in it. Activities put pressure *directly* on my body and my soul, on me personally.

I notice that when I am stretched too thin with things, I become unbalanced in other areas in order to compensate. I think more about eating and buying things in order to balance my pressured life. These compensations don't really work.

What does work? Getting rid of activities, hard as that may be. Dropping classes, meetings, shopping trips, church and charity activities, television shows, or whatever it is that is "too much." Then balance, sanity, and most of all, satisfaction is restored.

"Wherefore do ye spend . . . your labor for that which satis-fieth not?" (Isaiah 55:2)

Spiritual Reflection

Lord, when the glare and harshness of activities blinds and weakens me, lead me to a cool green glade of stillness where I may restore my vision and strength.

Personal Reflection

Dignity

"Free at last, free at last. Praise God Almighty, I'm free at last." The woman's voice was husky with feeling as she said that about her year-long uphill climb out of disorder. "It's so good," she said sincerely, "to be free."

I need to remember I can have that freedom, too. I want to live a life unfettered by clutter. How many of us want to be able to say that!

Surely the woman whose husband left her wants to say it. They recently reconciled, but he couldn't move back in because there was no room in the cluttered house. Surely the woman who, with her husband, owned three houses as real estate investments wants to say it. They could not put the houses on the market because they were being used as storage sheds for her overwhelming possessions.

These are interesting women of dignity—but women who are bound and longing to be "free at last." And they, with all of us, can be.

Spiritual Reflection

Lord, what a word, freedom. *As I thirst for it, let me settle for nothing less.*

Personal Reflection

Vision

I was building a sand castle on the beach by the lake when the baby came up to "help" me. His little hands started to tear down the turrets and destroy the walls. I began making a sand sculpture for him to work on so he would leave my castle alone. I decided to make a sand turtle for him. We worked together. He loved piling the sand on the sculpture, but he never saw that it was a turtle just as he never noticed mine was a castle. He just piled sand, destroying the turtle sculpture with every unskilled handful. Eventually, he walked through my castle, destroying what he never knew existed.

God, who is sculpting my life, must look at my feeble efforts in much the same way. He is doing something wonderful and meaningful while I am often just doing. Is my messiness part of my undoing of his design in my life, my mindless doing, my destroying of much that could be good, if I just had the eyes to see?

Spiritual Reflection

O, God, open my eyes to the wonderful design you have for my life. Help me to quit tearing down your building. Along the shoreline of life, give me vision for the beauty and grace possible in my life.

Personal Reflection

# COURAGE

Be strong and courageous. Do not be afraid or terrified because of them, for the Lord your God goes with you; he will never leave you nor forsake you.

—Deuteronomy 31:6 NIV

Priorities

There will be times when my family seems to be working against me. I will remember that they, like me, have their own problems. If they are disorganized and uncooperative, it is because they are losing in their own struggles.

I will treat myself with respect and not let them destroy the order that is so important to me. I will also treat them with respect. I will attempt to speak with kindness and calmness and mean it. I will set a gracious tone. I will be tolerant of their faults. As my thinking and actions return to normalcy, others will be affected.

Becoming orderly is only one part of building a good life. I can be neat and still have a messed up life if I am angry or hurtful to others.

Spiritual Reflection

Lord, help me to remember that a gracious life, not a neat environment, is my goal.

Personal Reflection

_____

_____

_____

_____

_____

_____

Focus

One reason it is so hard to see the way out of clutter and confusion is that the whole situation is so full of contradictions.

On the one hand I am a perfectionist, but my house is just the opposite. Sometimes I think I am lazy, but at others I feel I work much harder than other people. I take my family seriously and try to improve it. Yet the mess I allow hinders my family seriously.

The answer is this. I am pulling my life forward on a day-to-day basis. This part is visible to me and to others. The hidden part is that at the same time I am pulling forward, I am also pushing myself and my house backward. This is obscure because it is a matter of attitudes and decisions of which I and others are unaware.

Spiritual Reflection

"Every wise woman buildeth her house; but the foolish plucketh it down with her hands" (Proverbs 14:1).

Personal Reflection

Beauty

The Biltmore Hotel in Coral Gables, Florida, is a beautiful and historic landmark built in the Moorish style. It has recently been restored and now is breathtaking with its star-studded blue vaulted ceilings, marble columns and floors, rock pools, Moorish stone statuary, and marvelously interesting chandeliers.

Before it was restored, however, it had fallen on hard times and had been converted to a V.A. hospital during World War II. A dropped acoustical ceiling was put in. Linoleum was put over the marble floors, and partitions for offices were nailed onto the marble columns. The beauty was hidden in the trappings of hospital life. Years passed.

When they removed the dropped ceiling and linoleum, imagine their joy and surpise at what they found. The beauty had been protected by these coverings.

Like the Biltmore, my house holds beauty, covered and hidden by clutter and disorder. As I roll those back, what wonderful loveliness will emerge? I can't wait to see!

Spiritual Reflection

Lord, excite me with the possibilities of beauty within my house.

Personal Reflection

_____

_____

_____

_____

_____

Courage

No one, except someone who has experienced it, understands the fear of loss that some of us encounter when we consider eliminating possessions.

Many people think that those who endured the losses of the Great Depression are the ones who become "pack rats." However, I know I was not even born during that time, and I have the same characteristics.

Many times this "pack rat" syndrome begins after people lose someone very special to them in death. Somehow the shock of that loss triggers a latent fear of losing anything. Now they put a dam on the flow of anything from their houses.

This causes a messy house. And that's the greatest loss of all. The word for the day is *courage*, to face the fear of loss.

"A man's life does not consist in the abundance of his possessions" (Luke 12:15 NIV).

Spiritual Reflection

Lord, why do I fear loss in the future so much that I am willing to lose the joy of present living in order to prepare for it?

Personal Reflection

Patience

It is easy and comfortable to place the blame for the messy state of our houses on other people and other things. There is usually enough truth to that approach to make it acceptable. Others often are a big part of the mess in the house.

Yet somehow I feel that even so, the catalyst for change lies within me. As I come into line with my own priorities, strange and wonderful things begin to happen. When I dissipate my energies by focusing on others and their faults, nothing seems to happen. Managing others frequently promotes only resentment and hostility.

Let me concentrate on myself as I keep my goals spotlighted, keep my priorities in line, find balance in my excesses in life, and seek the inner peace that can be mine; the insanity of chaos around me will begin to melt in the warmth of my inner balance.

Spiritual Reflection

Lord, my soul pants for harmony in my life. I suspect it can only come from you through me. Keep me from looking to others for it.

Personal Reflection

Dignity

One of the distinguishing characteristics that sets successful average housekeepers apart from those who are either extremely messy or extremely neat is that the successful, average housekeeper seems to have an upbeat confidence about the future.

This optimistic outlook keeps her from feeling she has to keep scraps and useless junk just in case they will be needed in the future. Her positive outlook makes it possible, for instance, for her to read magazines and then let them go, because she is confident that more equally interesting magazines will take their places.

When I have this confident attitude it gives me a great deal of freedom. A feeling that the future will be somehow hostile causes me to barricade myself with my possessions. Confidence opens my life to the flow of good things.

"She is clothed with strength and dignity; she can laugh at the days to come" (Proverbs 31:25 NIV).

Spiritual Reflection

Lord, give me that confidence so that I will not fearfully cling to all the flotsam and jetsam of life in order to get courage.

Personal Reflection

Vision

The funny part about breaking free of the compulsion of messiness is how much resistance to change I find in myself. When I know I am a Messie, at least I know that I am something. If I were not a Messie, who would I be?

Messiness helps me avoid living responsibly as an adult. "I can't do such because I am messy," I tell myself. Messiness gives me a place to hang my unhappiness. I don't have to deal with the deficiencies that being a Messie masks. If I were not messy, I might find that I was still unhappy. Then I would have to deal with becoming healthy in other areas.

Messiness gives other people who know about my problem a way to relate to me. They criticize me and put me down. They try to help me. Maybe they like me only because I am needy. If I weren't messy, would they still fool with me? Messiness makes me unique. I am a little offbeat, eccentric, sort of special because of it. If I were like everyone else, I might be dull. Messiness is something to fight against on a daily basis so that I always have the excitement of either winning or losing. If I weren't messy, what would I think about?

Curing the messiness may end up being the easy part.

Spiritual Reflection

O Lord, I thought it was just a matter of dealing with clutter in the house. Now I suspect I may have debris in my heart that needs to be addressed. I need your help. Badly.

Personal Reflection

 PATIENCE

Be still before the Lord and wait patiently for him; . . .
do not fret—it leads only to evil.

—Psalms 37:7,8 NIV

Priorities

Pine forests need fire in order to prosper. The fire burns away competing trees, leaving more room for the fire-resistant pines. It also spreads pine cone seeds. Fire is not easy on the pines, but in the end they benefit from it.

I would never have deliberately chosen the heat and pain of having the problem of messiness. Perhaps, however, like the pine forest I can profit from my pain.

Messiness is a symptom of less obvious factors working in my life. Without the problem of disorganization, which demands attention, I probably would never have worked on finding my faults, recognizing my strengths, or clarifying my goals in life.

In the final analysis, I may be able to see through my struggles that this problem is a gift from God's gracious hand.

Spiritual Reflection

Father, help me not to miss the lessons in my pain. Use the fire of messiness that scorches me daily to burn off the faults that fuel it. Above all, use my struggles with disorder to help me grow.

Personal Reflection

Focus

Somewhere along the way I must face one of the chief hindrances in my program of change—inconsistency. It is important that I realize that inconsistency will be there. It is part of the human condition. It is particularly a part of the human condition of a disorganized person.

Inconsistency will be a part of my program of change. I will go forward it is true. It is also true that I will go backward as well. There will be ups and downs. If I don't expect these times, they will distract and discourage me.

When the down times come, it is important that I just keep doing something, working whatever part of the program I can until the up times come. Over time, through good and bad, change will come.

Spiritual Reflection

Lord, help me to keep plowing forward through the troughs and crests of change.

Personal Reflection

Beauty

Perhaps the hardest part of struggling with clutter is that it pulls our attention so down to earth. Because the house is disorganized and distracting, it requires much of my attention just to negotiate through it and make progress on a day-to-day basis.

I feel like a person walking down a muddy road trying to look at a beautiful sunset. My eyes search the mud, looking for the higher drier spots. I must avoid the ruts and puddles. The effort in struggling forward takes all my vision. Before me I know is the beauty of sun and clouds, glowing and dancing together. The beauty is there, but I cannot make it mine because I must concentrate all my efforts on walking across the mud.

And so the beauty passes in life, while I with my eyes on the clutter wander painfully through it. I miss the beauty that could be my experience.

Spiritual Reflection

Lord, this is my life! Don't let it pass with nothing but mud.

Personal Reflection

Courage

Two images keep recurring in Messie conversations and letters. One is the image of fire, and the other is of drowning. Messies devoutly desire some outside force to come and take away the awful burden of the responsibility of the clutter. "If only a fire would burn it all away and I could start over," they think. The Messie unwittingly clings so tightly to the unwanted, yet beloved, junk that only a fire can burn it away.

The image of drowning is sometimes accompanied by a picture, self-drawn, of the Messie being engulfed by clutter. Sometimes debris covers up the whole Messie until only one arm is seen flailing helplessly out from the pile. The image is similar to an overeater drowning in chocolate. The sinking Messie is going down for the last time.

Helpless is the word that unites these two images. The Messie feels helpless to do anything about her situation.

The first thing the Messie needs to do is to find herself. Who is she? Does she have a voice? Does she have a self? Is she a real person? If the answer is "Yes" to these questions, then there is hope for change.

Spiritual Reflection

O God, make me the person I was created to be. You already know who I am. Now let me seek and find myself among the debris.

Personal Reflection

Patience

Nothing brings as much serenity to me as the idea of taking care of myself and putting that idea to work. I used to think I was taking care of myself by keeping mindlessly busy with activities and by gathering loads of junk. I had some inkling of my need to take care of myself, but I was missing it by a mile. All I got out of that way of life was a frazzled schedule, a tired body, a house full of junk, and a sense of confusion about why I was so unsatisfied with how I was living.

Part of the reason I was so unsatisfied is that I was trying to "do" for others and save for others just in case they might need something. I had such a grandiose attitude. I would take care of others because I knew more than they did.

Now I respect others enough to let them do for themselves whatever their decisions tell them they need. I have a more humble attitude. Now I try to tune into my own needs. One of the nicest ways I meet my own needs is by keeping an orderly house. Somehow when I am serenely caring for myself and my needs are met, I am available to truly help others if they should ask for my aid.

Spiritual Reflection

God, deliver me from busybodiness. Grant me serenity. From that will flow order in my life and wisdom in relating to other lives.

Personal Reflection

Dignity

Overcoming my own disorder is very hard. Doing it while living with someone who is messy and not overcoming it is very, very hard.

I must remember several things if I am not going to let this situation scuttle my plans for change. The first thing I must remember is that this person may be suffering and trying more than I can realize. If I have been more successful than he has, I should be grateful for my own progress.

I must also remember to show respect for his approach where it involves his own life. I will not deny him the path of failure or recovery.

The third thing I will keep in mind is not to deny myself the order and balance that I desire. In those mutually shared areas of our lives and homes, some plan will have to be made that does not compromise my recovery.

Spiritual Reflection

Lord, ordering the things of my life seems so much easier than ordering the relationships. But both are hard.

Personal Reflection

_____

_____

_____

_____

_____

_____

Vision

A man walked by a construction site where several men were working. "What are you doing?" he asked the first man. "I'm laying bricks," he replied, annoyed that the man could not see the obvious and was bothering him with stupid questions. He asked the second man the same question and the reply was, "I am building a wall." Then he asked a third man and the reply came back, "I am building a cathedral for the glory of God." All were doing the same thing but what a difference it made in how they viewed their work.

I can look at my house in the same way. I can think, "I am picking up junk. What a drag." Or I can say to myself, "I am creating a lovely environment for myself and my family to grow in." I can hate unloading and loading the dishwasher and washing and folding clothes. Or I can see that I am preparing the stage on which I and those I love can live our lives in a dignified way.

My organizational life is not just mindless movement of stuff from one place to another. It is living, loving, and building graciousness. In the end, perhaps what we are really doing is building in our homes a cathedral for the glory of God.

Spiritual Reflection

God, grant me the vision to see beyond the mundane to the divine and the insight to know that more is going on than meets the eye.

Personal Reflection

DIGNITY

She is clothed with strength and dignity; she can laugh at the days to come.

—Proverbs 31:25 NIV

Priorities

Relapsing. Why does it happen? There are probably many reasons. Sometimes I get too tired because I overschedule or emergencies arise. Or sometimes I misjudge what I can do.

But there is a kind of relapsing that is not so easy to handle. It is the soul-wrenching, hard core messiness that flows from a disturbed heart. If I slip into self-recrimination and my self-esteem begins to sink, the house is the first symptom of my illness of heart. If I become depressed about my life or begin to feel sorry for myself, clutter is the result. Others drink, go on buying binges, overeat, gamble, or whatever. I clutter. I use clutter to comfort myself, to distract myself, to punish myself, to affirm that I am indeed unworthy to live a peaceful and dignified life. In some kind of mindless way I try to use disorder to solve my problem.

But it doesn't work. When I use clutter in this way, I am scratching where it does not itch. Only solutions that address the heart can touch my problem.

Spiritual Reflection

Great God, somehow I think I am not so much on a housekeeping quest as on a spiritual one. How does a pile of junk relate to my inner needs? I don't really know, but I sense that my heart and my house are related. Lord of the heart, meet me at the point of my need.

Personal Reflection

Focus

I need to remember that my house and the things in it exist for me. I do not exist for the house and its contents. I don't have a responsibility to do things to maintain them if they don't benefit me. Somehow I don't always keep this in view.

From now on, in relation to my house, I will remember that it exists to meet my needs. If there is something in the house that causes me a problem I don't have a responsibility to continue it.

This is not easy because that pile of papers, that awkward furniture arrangement, that strange storage organization, all were my ideas to begin with. I arranged things this way for what I thought was my benefit, but they didn't work for my good.

When I change I will do it with an overall goal in mind: What is really good for me?

Spiritual Reflection

Lord, keep my focus on my own needs when it comes to the house. Somehow it keeps slipping away to old ways of thinking. Keep me focused right.

Personal Reflection

_____

_____

_____

_____

_____

_____

Beauty

It is a blessing to have good books on household organizing available. I learn many new things from them and am reminded of many important things that I already know. They challenge me and help me set new goals. They give me how-to's that I would not have thought of myself.

As I read these books, however, it is important for me to be sure I am ready to apply the ideas I read about. My mind must have good ground for the seed to grow. Fear, shame, and guilt must be cleared out so the seeds of order, beauty, and harmony may grow.

Disorder and order both spring from the heart.

Spiritual Reflection

Lord, grant me freedom from the hidden mess in my heart so order may take its place.

Personal Reflection

_____

_____

_____

_____

_____

_____

_____

_____

Courage

One of the most powerful tools for change is a Messies Anonymous support group. If I am not now in a group, I will consider joining together with others who are working to improve their disorganized lives.

A glowing coal will soon burn out if it is separated from the burning pile of coals. If I am in a group when the cold winds of discouragement blow across my life and cool my desire for change, I can draw renewed warmth from those in my group. If I am all alone, it is easy to lose my motivation.

Perhaps there is a group in my area. If not, I will seek out one or more others in my community who may be just waiting for this kind of help themselves. Together we will search for the motivation, strength, and insight needed in that hardest of all human endeavors—change.

Spiritual Reflection

"Two are better than one; because they have a good reward for their labor. For if they fall, the one will lift up his fellow: but woe to him that is alone when he falleth: for he hath not another to help him up" (Ecclesiastes 4:9–10).

Personal Reflection

Patience

"The fruit of the Spirit [of God] is . . . temperance," says the Bible (Galatians 5:22). It is not surprising then that as I set my mind to seek and follow God I will find myself becoming more like the dictionary definition of temperance. I become "self-restrained in conduct, expression, indulgence of the appetites. . . ."

A woman who was compulsively neat found normalcy as she followed the spiritual path. The second step of the Alcoholics Anonymous Twelve-Step program says that we "came to believe that a power greater than ourselves could restore us to sanity." Whether a person is compulsively neat or in my case, compulsively messy, looking for help through that "Power greater than ourselves" will bring what the Bible calls temperance, or what Alcoholics Anonymous calls sanity.

Spiritual Reflection

Lord, I need temperance, sanity, or whatever it may be called. I need relief—permanent, blessed release—from the disorder that dogs my life.

Personal Reflection

Dignity

I have many resources to help me make the changes that I want to make in my life. I have books available. I have tapes, meditation. And, if I wish, I may join or start a self-help support group. The principles of this program are open to me.

Why do I not always take full advantage of these aids? Is it because changing to an organized life-style is not really that important to me? Do I feel that I do not really deserve the beautiful and harmonious life they will bring? Am I afraid of peace and control because I think that kind of life will be boring or will put too much responsibility on my shoulders? Perhaps I use this terrible life-style to punish myself for some guilt I feel.

I must lift my head above the fog of these thoughts and follow the principles of focus, moderation, detachment, courage, and the other principles of this program in order to re-establish the sense of dignity that first gave me the hope of change.

Spiritual Reflection

Lord, keep me from dragging myself down. If I don't help myself there is no one else who will do it for me.

Personal Reflection

_____

_____

_____

_____

_____

_____

Vision

I cannot lose weight for another person. I know that. I cannot stop drinking or smoking for another person. I know that. I cannot overcome drug use for another. Why then do I think that by nagging I can make someone else become neat?

Nothing is harder than for one person who has found change in life to see others who continue their destructive ways and do not seem interested in changing. The temptation is to nag, browbeat, and harass. This just brings verbal clutter into the house. Harsh words only stir up resentment and discouragement. They kill respect and love. They degrade me as I use them. Would I have wanted anyone to do that to me when I was floundering?

All I can do is to maintain my own vision of change. I can change myself and my life on a daily basis. Perhaps others will be attracted to change by my example.

Spiritual Reflection

Lord, you know my temptation to unleash harsh words in my frustration. This only causes more. Give me clarity of thought to remember this.

Personal Reflection

# VISION

Where there is no vision, the people perish.
—Proverbs 29:18

Priorities

I will use the tools available to me to change my thinking. From that, my life will change.

I will listen to affirmative talk, read helpful books, write my goals and meet with others who face the same struggles I do.

If things improve, I will continue to use the tools so that I can maintain that change. If things don't improve, I will still continue to use the tools until they do.

I won't allow myself to be encouraged or discouraged away from the Messies Anonymous program. If I find I have drifted away, I will not spend energy feeling guilty, but will pick up the tools and return to the daily business of change.

Spiritual Reflection

Lord, give me detachment from my own fluctuating emotions. Give me faith that if I use the tools I have for change that the change I yearn for will come.

Personal Reflection

_____

_____

_____

_____

_____

_____

_____

Focus

The wisest man who ever lived tells us: "Catch for us the foxes, the little foxes that ruin the vineyards, our vineyards that are in bloom" (Song of Solomon 2:15).

It is the *little* foxes I need to watch out for. An interruption here, a distraction there, a careless plan that takes more time than I realized. In the end, the vineyard of my time schedule is spoiled.

Solomon encourages me to catch the foxes that spoil the vine. It is only when I become aware of the little rascals, what they are and when they come, that I can even begin to think of catching them.

Today I will watch to see what little things spoil my time schedule. If I value the vineyard of an ordered and successful life, those foxes must be caught.

Spiritual Reflection

Lord, help me spot those little foxes, so cute and appealing. Help me see them for what they are and eliminate them from the vineyard of my life.

Personal Reflection

Beauty

Thoreau is famous for his statement that most men "live lives of quiet desperation." In an attempt to avoid such a fate he lived alone on Walden Pond with only the basics of life from 1845 to 1847. He went to focus on what was really important in life. He wrote. "I went to the woods because I wanted to live deliberately . . . and not, when I came to die, discover that I had not lived. I did not wish to live what was not life, living is so dear. . . ."

In my hurry, clutter, and yes, desperation to cram all of life I can into the time I have here, I may well find when I look back that I have not really lived life. I have just manipulated time and things. Jesus said that a man's life does not consist in the abundance of things he possesses. Like Thoreau I must pull back, away from that distraction, and live deliberately so that I may truly live before I die.

Spiritual Reflection

Lord, take me to my Walden Pond until I know the truth of how to live a life with meaning.

Personal Reflection

Courage

No one knows how much fear is buried deep down inside of me when it comes to the subject of organization. Sometimes I don't even realize it myself because I bury it under such a layer of intellectualizing.

Frequently I say that I am too busy to organize or I am too tired to get to some job. I rationalize that need to keep this or that for the future and so I can't throw it out. What's closer to the truth is that I am afraid to tackle these organizing jobs, many of which involve decision making. I am afraid that if I move something from where it is now, it will be lost permanently. I am afraid that if I get rid of something now I will need it later. I am afraid that I won't be able to figure out how to handle the stuff and so will have only a new set of piles.

Organizing techniques will begin to help me only when I am not afraid to use them.

Spiritual Reflection

Lord, help me find my way through and then out of this fear that is like an invisible chain keeping me from the order and beauty I crave.

Personal Reflection

Patience

It is both comforting and troubling to think that the suffering I experience because of the clutter and confusion in my life may be the result of my own thoughts and attitudes. The thoughts and attitudes that have gotten me in this fix are not necessarily bad. They just do not work in my circumstances. Or it may be I take good ideas and overdo them to the point where they cause me trouble.

I will stop blaming my upbringing, my present circumstances, or other people. There are many people leading orderly, harmonious lives who have the same circumstances or worse. I will concentrate on changing my thoughts, knowing that the power to change is within my control.

Spiritual Reflection

Lord, you have put the responsibility of my life in my hands. I go on record today accepting that responsibility as fully mine.

Personal Reflection

Dignity

One of the most important concepts for me to remember is that I am responsible for nurturing myself well. In the past I have tried to take care of myself by gathering up lots of junk in case I needed something. I have left stuff lying around the house so I would have easy access to what I needed. I found a strange kind of comfort in having clutter around me. But I found that although it promised nurturing, it brought only frustration.

Now that I realize this, I will begin to be good to myself by letting this old way of life go. I will be good to myself—really good to myself—by gathering order and neatness around me and finding real comfort from them.

Spiritual Reflection

Lord, help me see where my comfort really lies. And help me remember that I am important enough to deserve it.

Personal Reflection

Vision

Down in the bowels of the O'Hare airport in Chicago, one of the busiest in the world, is a chapel. To get to the service on Sunday one must go to the basement level and travel through long gray halls until, happily, the lighted chapel sign appears. It would be scary down there if it weren't for a guard.

Above is the bustle of commerce. Below is a haven of worship, peace, and reflection on issues that go far beyond commerce for travelers and personnel. Finding it there is like finding a cave in a storm.

In the bustle and rush of busy living, it is beneficial in a way that is hard to understand except by experiencing it. It is important to take time to find, on a daily basis, the chapel of my own soul. Strengthened, I return above to jobs, housework, and caring for others. Are things different for my having gone there? Yes, in ways more significant because they are unseen, my life is benefited.

Spiritual Reflection

Great God, be pleased to meet me in the chapel of my soul. Shine on me there your reflection and let it light all my day.

Personal Reflection

The Twelve Steps of Messies Anonymous

1. We admitted we were powerless over clutter and disorganization—that our lives had become unmanageable.
2. We came to believe that a Power greater than ourselves could restore us to sanity.
3. We made a decision to turn our will and our lives to the care of God as we understood Him.
4. We made a searching and fearless moral inventory of ourselves.
5. We admitted to God, to ourselves, and to another human being the exact nature of our wrongs.
6. We were entirely ready to have God remove all these defects of character.
7. We humbly asked Him to remove our shortcomings.
8. We made a list of all persons we had harmed, and became willing to make amends to them all.
9. We made direct amends to such people whenever possible, except when to do so would injure them or others.
10. We continued to take personal inventory, and when we were wrong promptly admitted it.
11. We sought Him through prayer and meditation to improve our conscious contact with God as we understood Him, praying only for the knowledge of His will for us and power to carry that out.
12. Having had a spiritual awakening as the result of these steps, we tried to carry this message to others who suffer from disorganization in their lives, and to practice these principles in all our affairs.

The Twelve Steps of Alcoholics Anonymous

1. We admitted we were powerless over alcohol—that our lives had become unmanageable.
2. Came to believe that a Power greater than ourselves could restore us to sanity.
3. Made a decision to turn our will and our lives over to the care of God as we understood Him.
4. Made a searching and fearless moral inventory of ourselves.
5. Admitted to God, to ourselves, and to another human being the exact nature of our wrongs.
6. Were entirely ready to have God remove all these defects of character.
7. Humbly asked Him to remove our shortcomings.
8. Made a list of all persons we had harmed, and became willing to make amends to them all.
9. Made direct amends to such people wherever possible, except when to do so would injure them or others.

10. Continued to take personal inventory and when we were wrong promptly admitted it.
11. Sought through prayer and meditation to improve our conscious contact with God as we understood Him, praying only for knowledge of His will for us and the power to carry that out.
12. Having had a spiritual awakening as the result of these steps, we tried to carry this message to alcoholics, and to practice these principles in all our affairs.

The Twelve Traditions of Messies Anonymous

1. Our common welfare should come first; personal progress depends upon unity.
2. For our group purpose there is but one ultimate authority—a loving Higher Power. Our leaders are but trusted servants; they do not govern.
3. The only requirement for membership in an M.A. group is a desire for freedom from clutter and a disorganized lifestyle. Any such group may call itself a Messies Anonymous group provided that, as a group, they have no other affiliation.
4. Each group should be autonomous except when action taken would be inconsistent with program principles and guidelines, as described in M.A. literature.
5. Each group has but one primary purpose—to help those who desire a sanely organized lifestyle.
6. An M.A. group ought never endorse, finance, or lend the M.A. name to any outside enterprise, lest problems of money, property, and prestige divert us from our primary purpose.
7. Every M.A. group ought to be self-supporting, declining outside contributions.
8. M.A. should remain forever nonprofessional, but our service centers may employ special workers.
9. M.A. as such ought never be organized; but we may create service boards or committees directly responsible to those they serve.

10. M.A. has no opinion on outside issues; hence the M.A. name ought never be drawn into public controversy.
11. Our public relations policy is based on attraction rather than promotion; we need always maintain personal anonymity at the level of press, television, radio and films.
12. Anonymity is the spiritual foundation of all our traditions, ever reminding us to place principles over personalities.

The Twelve Traditions of Alcoholics Anonymous

1. Our common welfare should come first; personal recovery depends upon A.A. unity.
2. For our group purpose there is but one ultimate authority—a loving God as he may express Himself in our group conscience. Our leaders are but trusted servants; they do not govern.
3. The only requirement for A.A. membership is a desire to stop drinking.
4. Each group should be autonomous except in matters affecting other groups or A.A. as a whole.
5. Each group has but one primary purpose—to carry its message to the alcoholic who still suffers.
6. An A.A. group ought never endorse, finance or lend the A.A. name to any related facility or outside enterprise, lest problems of money, property and prestige divert us from our primary purpose.
7. Every A.A. group ought to be fully self-supporting, declining outside contributions.
8. Alcoholics Anonymous should remain forever non-professional, but our service centers may employ special workers.

9. A.A., as such, ought never be organized; but we may create service boards or committees directly responsible to those they serve.
10. Alcoholics Anonymous has no opinion on outside issues; hence the A.A. name ought never be drawn into public controversy.
11. Our public relations policy is based on attraction rather than promotion; we need always maintain personal anonymity at the level of press, radio, films and T.V.
12. Anonymity is the spiritual foundation of all our traditions, ever reminding us to place principles over personalities.

MORE HELP FROM MESSIES ANONYMOUS

If you would like a free Messies Anonymous sample newsletter with information about obtaining the complete Messies Anonymous Flipper Kit and other helps available from Messies Anonymous, write to:

MESSIES ANONYMOUS™
5025 S.W. 114 Avenue
Miami, Florida 33165

Sandra Felton's research on the "why" and "how to" of the problem of messiness continues. She welcomes your comments on this book and any relevant stories from your life which relate to your struggle with the house, whether successful or not.